QUICK LANGUAGES

MULTI-LANGUAGE PHRASEBOOK COLLECTION

AMERICAN
BOOK GROUP

ENGLISH-ITALIAN
ITALIAN-ENGLISH

GET THE AUDIOVISUAL AND
INTERACTIVE CONTENT AT
QuickLanguages.com

QUICK LANGUAGES

MULTI-LANGUAGE PHRASEBOOK COLLECTION

SPEAK ANY LANGUAGE NOW!

WHAT IS QUICK LANGUAGES?

Did you know that we only use about 1,000 words in our everyday vocabulary? The same goes for any language! So, mastering a digital phrasebook with interactive pronunciation tools is a smart alternative to long and expensive language instruction.

Quick Languages is an interactive phrasebook that introduces you to the 12 predominant world languages all in one convenient drop-down menu. Designed for visual, auditory, and kinesthetic learners alike, it is simple, affordable, and effective.

Own the potential of connecting with over 3 billion people!

QUICK LANGUAGES

MULTI-LANGUAGE PHRASEBOOK COLLECTION

SPEAK ANY LANGUAGE NOW!

QUICK LANGUAGES PHRASEBOOK COLLECTION
AVAILABLE TITLES

1. ENGLISH-SPANISH & SPANISH-ENGLISH
2. ENGLISH-ITALIAN & ITALIAN-ENGLISH
3. ENGLISH-FRENCH & FRENCH-ENGLISH
4. ENGLISH-GERMAN & GERMAN-ENGLISH
5. ENGLISH-PORTUGUESE & PORTUGUESE-ENGLISH
6. ENGLISH-CHINESE & CHINESE-ENGLISH
7. ENGLISH-ARABIC & ARABIC-ENGLISH
8. ENGLISH-JAPANESE & JAPANESE-ENGLISH
9. ENGLISH-KOREAN & KOREAN-ENGLISH
10. ENGLISH-RUSSIAN & RUSSIAN-ENGLISH
11. ENGLISH-TURKISH & TURKISH-ENGLISH

GET THE AUDIOVISUAL AND
INTERACTIVE CONTENT AT
QuickLanguages.com

LEARN MORE ABOUT OUR BOOKS AT:
americanbookgroup.com

AMERICAN
BOOK GROUP

COMPANION ONLINE COURSE
quicklanguages.com

Quick Languages: 1,000 Key Words and Expressions Phrasebook
ENGLISH-ITALIAN & ITALIAN-ENGLISH

Author's Copyright © 2023 Quick Languages
Publisher's Copyright © 2023 AMERICAN BOOK GROUP

To request permissions, contact the publisher at info@trialtea.com

Paperback ISBN: 978-1-681655-92-5

Library of Congress Control Code: 2023932203

First paperback edition: April 2023

Edited by Gregorio García
Cover art by Natalia Urbano
Layout by Esmeralda Riveros & Pancho Guijarro

Printed in the USA

American Book Group
americanbookgroup.com

INDEX OF CONTENTS

1,000 KEY WORDS AND EXPRESSIONS

English / Italian - Italian / English

Keep practicing at:
QuickLanguages.com

1. Greetings
/ Saluti

Hi! / Hello!	**Ciao / Salve!**
Good morning	**Buon giorno!**
Good afternoon	**Buon giorno!**
Good evening / Good night	**Buona sera! / buona notte!**
How are you doing?	**Come stai?**
Fine	**Bene**
Very well	**Molto bene**
Thank you / Thanks	**Grazie**
Thank you very much	**Grazie mille**
You're welcome	**Prego**
Fine, thank you	**Va bene, grazie**
And you?	**E tu?**
See you	**A presto**
See you later	**A presto!Ciao!**
See you tomorrow	**A domani**
Goodbye	**Arrivederci!**
Bye	**Ciao!**

2. Introductions and Courtesy Expressions / **Presentazione ed espressioni di cortesia**

What is your name?	**Come si chiama?**
My name is ...	**Mi chiamo...**
Who are you?	**Chi è lei?**
I am ...	**Io sono....**
Who is he / she?	**Chi è lui?/ Chi è lei?**
He is ... / She is ...	**Lui è.../lei è....**
Nice to meet you / Pleased to meet you	**Piacere di conoscerla**
Nice to meet you, too	**Anche per me è un piacere di conoscerla!**
It's my pleasure	**Il piacere è mio**
Excuse me	**La prego di scusarmi**
Please	**Per favore/prego**
One moment, please	**Un attimo, prego**
Welcome	**Benvenuto!**
Go ahead	**Prego, s'accomodi**
Can you repeat, please?	**Potrebbe ripetere, per favore?**
I don't understand	**Non capisco**
I understand a little	**Capisco un po'**
Can you speak more slowly, please?	**Potrebbe parlare più lentamente per favore?**
Do you speak Spanish?	**Parla spagnolo?**
How do you say hello in Spanish?	**Come si dice "salve" in spagnolo?**
What does it mean?	**Che cosa significa questo?**
I speak Spanish a little	**Parlo un po' lo spagnolo.**

3. Ways to Address a Person / Forme per rivolgersi ad una persona

Madam / Ma'am	**Signora**
Miss	**Signorina**
Ms.	**Sig.na**
Mr.	**Sig**
Mrs.	**Sig.ra**
Sir	**Signore**
Dr.	**Dottore**

4. The Articles / L'articolo determinativo e indeterminativo

The	**Il, lo, l' / la, l' / i, gli / le**
The car	**La macchina**
The cars	**Le macchine**
The house	**La casa**
The houses	**Le case**
A	**Un,uno / una, un'**
A car	**Una macchina**
A house	**Una casa**
An	**Un' (quando la parola in femminile comincia con una vocale)**
An elephant	**Un elefante**
An apple	**Una mela**
Some	**Dei, delle, degli**
Some cars	**Delle macchine**
Some houses	**Delle case**

5. The Subject Pronouns / Pronomi personali

I	**Io**
You	**Tu**
He	**Lui**
She	**Lei**
It	**Ø**
We	**Noi**
You	**Voi**
They	**Loro**

6. The Possessive Adjectives / Gli Aggettivi possessivi

My	**Mio/a**
Your	**Tuo/a**
His	**Suo/a**
Her	**Suo/a**
Its	**Suo/a**
Our	**Nostro/a**
Your	**Vostro/a**
Their	**Loro**
My car	**La mia macchina**
Your book	**Il tuo libro**
His TV	**Il suo televisore**
Our house	**La nostra casa**

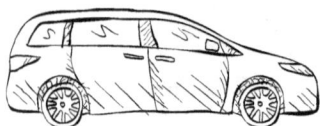

7. The Demonstrative Adjectives / Gli Aggettivi dimostrativi

This	Questo/questa
This book	Questo libro
This shirt	Questa camicia
These	Questi/queste
These books	Questi libri
These shirts	Queste camicie
That	Quel,quello/quella
That table	Quel tavolo
That car	Quella macchina
Those	Quei, quegli/quelle
Those tables	Quei tavoli
Those cars	Quelle macchine

8. The Possessive Pronouns / I pronomi possessivi

Mine	Mio, mia miei, mie
Yours	Tuo, tua, tuoi, tue
His	Suo, suoi, sue
Hers	Sua, suoi, sue
Its	Suo, suoi, sue
Ours	Nostro/a, nostri, nostre
Yours	Vostro/a, votri, vostre
Theirs	Loro
The car is mine	La macchina è mia
The book is yours	Il libro è tuo
That TV is his	Questo è il suo televisore
This house is ours	Questa è la nostra casa

9. The Cardinal Numbers
/ I numeri cardinali

0 / Zero	**Zero**
1 / One	**Uno**
2 / Two	**Due**
3 / Three	**Tre**
4 / Four	**Quattro**
5 / Five	**Cinque**
6 / Six	**Sei**
7 / Seven	**Sette**
8 / Eight	**Otto**
9 / Nine	**Nove**
10 / Ten	**Dieci**
11 / Eleven	**Undici**
12 / Twelve	**Dodici**
13 / Thirteen	**Tredici**
14 / Fourteen	**Quattordici**
15 / Fifteen	**Quindici**
16 / Sixteen	**Sedici**
17 / Seventeen	**Diciasette**
18 / Eighteen	**Diciotto**
19 / Nineteen	**Diciannove**
20 / Twenty	**Venti**
21 / Twenty-one	**Ventuno**
30 / Thirty	**Trenta**
40 / Forty	**Quaranta**
50 / Fifty	**Cinquanta**
60 / Sixty	**Sessanta**

1. 2. 3. 4.
5. 6. 7. 8.
9. 0.

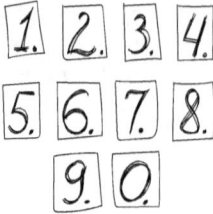

9. The Cardinal Numbers / I numeri cardinali

70 / Seventy	**Settanta**
80 / Eighty	**Ottanta**
90 / Ninety	**Novanta**
100 / One hundred	**Cento**
101 / One hundred and one	**Centuno**
200 / Two hundred	**Duecento**
300 / Three hundred	**Trecento**
400 / Four hundred	**Quattrocento**
500 / Five hundred	**Cinquecento**
600 / Six hundred	**Seicento**
700 / Seven hundred	**Settecento**
800 / Eight hundred	**Ottocento**
900 / Nine hundred	**Novecento**
1,000 / One thousand	**Mille**
10,000 / Ten thousand	**Diecimila**
100,000 / One hundred thousand	**Centomila**
1,000,000 / One million	**Un milione**
1,000,000,000 / One billion	**Un miliardo**
Forty-five (45)	**Quarantacinque**
One hundred and twenty-eight (128)	**Centoventotto**
One thousand nine hundred and sixty-three (1,963)	**Millenovecentosessantatre**
Six thousand and thirty-seven (6,037)	**Seimilatrentasette**
Eleven thousand (11,000)	**Undicimila**
Two hundred and seventy-nine thousand (279,000)	**Duecentosettantanovemila**
Two million (2,000,000)	**Duemilioni**

10. The Time
/ L'ora

The clock	**L'orologio da muro**
The watch	**L'orologio da polso**
What time is it?	**Che ore sono?**
It is ...	**Sono le...**
It is one o'clock (1:00)	**E' l'una**
It is two o'clock (2:00)	**Sono le due**
It is three fifteen / It is a quarter past three (3:15)	**Sono le tre e un quarto**
It is four thirty / It is half past four (4:30)	**Sono le quattro e mezza**
It is five forty-five / It is a quarter to six (5:45)	**Sono le cinque e quarantacinque/sono le sei meno quindici**
It is six fifty / It is ten to seven (6:50)	**Sono le sei e cinquanta/sono le sette meno dieci**
It is noon (12:00 P. M.)	**E' mezzoggiorno**
It is midnight (12:00 A. M.)	**E' mezzanotte**
In the morning	**La mattina**
In the afternoon	**Il pomeriggio**
In the evening	**La notte**
At night	**Durante la notte**
At what time is ...?	**A che ora è.../**
At what time is the concert?	**A che ora comincia il concerto?**
At ...	**Alle....**
At 7:10 P.M. (seven ten in the evening)	**Alle diciannove e dieci**

11. The Days of the Week
/ I giorni della settimana

Monday	**Lunedì**
Tuesday	**Martedì**
Wednesday	**Mercoledì**
Thursday	**Giovedì**
Friday	**Venerdì**
Saturday	**Sabato**
Sunday	**Domenica**
What day is today?	**Che giorno è oggi?**

12. The Months of the Year
/ I mesi dell'anno

January	**Gennaio**
February	**Febbraio**
March	**Marzo**
April	**Aprile**
May	**Maggio**
June	**Giugno**
July	**Luglio**
August	**Agosto**
September	**Settembre**
October	**Ottobre**
November	**Novembre**
December	**Dicembre**
What is today's date?	**Che data è oggi?**

13. The Weather
/ Il Tempo

Sunny	**Soleggiato**
Cloudy	**Nuvoloso**
Rainy	**Piovoso**
Humid	**Umido**
Dry	**Secco**
Cold	**Freddo**
Warm	**Caldo**
Hot	**Molto caldo**
Rain	**La pioggia**
Snow	**La neve**
How is the weather today?	**Che tempo fa oggi?**
It's nice	**Fa bel tempo**
It's sunny	**E' soleggiato**
It's cold in winter	**D'inverno fa freddo**
It's raining	**Piove**
It's snowing	**Nevica**
I am cold	**Ho freddo**

14. The Seasons
/ Le stagioni

Spring	**La primavera**
Summer	**L'estate**
Fall	**L'autunno**
Winter	**L'inverno**

15. The Colors
/ I colori

Yellow	**Giallo**
Red	**Rosso**
Blue	**Blu**
Green	**Verde**
Orange	**Arancione**
Brown	**Marrone**
Pink	**Rosa**
Purple	**Lilla**
Black	**Nero**
White	**Bianco**
Gray	**Grigio**
Light	**Chiaro**
Dark	**Scuro**
Light green	**Verde chiaro**
Orange book	**Un libro arancione**
Brown shoes	**Delle scarpe marroni**
My blouse is white	**La mia camicetta è bianca**
What color is...?	**Di che colore è**
What is your favorite color?	**Qual'è il tuo colore preferito?**

16. The Parts of the Face
/ Le Parti della Faccia

Cheek	**La guancia**
Chin	**Il mento**
Ear	**L'orecchio**
Eye	**L'occhio**
Forehead	**La fronte**
Hair	**I capelli**
Lips	**Le labbra**
Mouth	**La bocca**
Nose	**Il naso**
Skin	**La pelle**
Teeth	**I denti**
Tooth	**Il dente**
Blond / Blonde	**Biondo/bionda**
Brown	**Castano**
Gray	**Biancho**
Red hair	**Capelli rossi**
Long	**Lunghi**
Short	**Corti**
Straight	**Lisci**
Curly	**Ricci**
John is blond	**Giovanni è biondo**
Karen has long hair	**Karen ha i capelli lunghi**
He has green eyes	**Lui ha gli occhi verdi**
Her eyes are blue	**Lei ha gli occhi azzurri**
His eyes are big and brown	**Lui ha gli occhi grandi e marroni**

17. Essential Verbs
/ Verbi Essenziali

Be	**Essere**
Go	**Andare**
Come	**Venire**
Have	**Avere**
Get	**Prendere**
Help	**Aiutare**
Love	**Amare**
Like	**Piacere**
Want	**Volere**
Buy	**Comprare**
Sell	**Vendere**
Read	**Leggere**
Write	**Scrivere**
Drink	**Bere**
Eat	**Mangiare**
Open	**Aprire**
Close	**Chiudere**
Look at	**Guardare**
Look for	**Cercare**
Find	**Trovare**
Start	**Cominciare**
Stop	**Fermarsi**
Pull	**Tirare**

17. Essential Verbs
/ Verbi Essenziali

Push	**Spingere**
Send	**Inviare**
Receive	**Ricevere**
Turn on	**Accendere**
Turn off	**Speanere**
Listen to	**Ascoltare**
Speak	**Parlare**
Do	**Fare**
Drive	**Guidare**
Feel	**Sentire**
Know	**Sapere**
Leave	**Rimanere/uscire**
Live	**Vivere**
Make	**Preparare**
Meet	**Conoscere / Incontrare**
Need	**Avere bisogno**
Pay	**Pagare**
Play	**Giocare**
Remember	**Ricordare**
Repeat	**Ripetere**
Say	**Dire**
Sit	**Sedersi**
Sleep	**Dormire**

17. Essential Verbs / Verbi Essenziali

Study	**Studiare**
Take	**Prendere**
Think	**Pensare**
Understand	**Capire**
Wait	**Aspettare**
Watch	**Guardare/osservare**
There is	**C'è**
There are	**Ci sono**
I am tall	**Sono alto**
You are short	**Sono basso**
He is thin	**Lui è magro**
We are big	**Noi siamo grandi**
They are intelligent	**Loro sono intelligenti**
I am at home	**Sono a casa**
You are at school	**Loro sono a scuola**
We are at the store	**Noi siamo al negozio**
I get a prize	**Ho preso un premio**
I go to the movies	**Vado al cinema**
I have a nice car	**Ho un bella macchina**
I listen to the music	**Ascolto la musica**
I watch TV.	**Guardo la televisione**
I like this book	**Questo libro mi piace**
There are ten children in the park	**Nel parco ci sono dieci bambini**

18. Interrogative Words
/ Pronomi interrogativi

How many ...?	**Quanti/e...?**
How much...?	**Quanto/a...?**
How ...?	**Come...?**
What ...?	**Che cosa...?**
When ...?	**Quando...?**
Where ...?	**Dove...?**
Which ...?	**Quale...?**
Who ...?	**Chi...?**
Whose ...?	**Di chi...?**
Whom ...? / To whom ...?	**A chi...? Per chi...?**
Why ...?	**Perchè...?**
Because ...	**Perchè...**

19. Linking Words
/ Le congiunzioni

And	**E**
But	**Ma**
Or	**O**
Either ... or	**O...o**
Neither ... nor	**Nè...nè**
Yes	**Si**
No	**No**
So	**Allora**
While	**Mentre**

20. The Prepositions
/ Le preposizioni

About	**Circa**
Above	**Sopra**
Across	**Di fronte a**
At	**A, verso**
Behind	**Dietro**
Below	**Sotto**
Between	**Tra, fra**
By	**In**
Down	**In basso**
During	**Durante**
For	**Per**
From	**Di**
In	**In**
In front of	**Davanti**
Into	**Dentro**

20. The Prepositions
/ Le preposizioni

Near	**Vicino a**
Next to	**Di fianco**
Of	**A**
On	**A, sopra**
Out	**Fuori**
Over	**Sopra**
Per	**Per**
Through	**Attraverso**
To	**Verso**
Under	**Sotto**
Up	**Su**
With	**Con**
Without	**Senza**
The cat is in the box	**Il gatto è nella scatola**
The vase is on the table	**Il vaso è sulla tavola**
Somebody is at the door	**C'è qualcuno alla porta**

21. Giving Directions
/ Dare istruzioni

At the corner	all'angolo
Far	lontano
Near	Vicino
Go straight ahead	Vada dritto
Left	A sinistra
Right	A destra
Turn left	Giri a sinistra
Turn right	Giri a destra
Go straight one block	Vada dritto fino alla prossima strada
After the traffic light, turn right	Al semaforo giri a destra
How can I get to ...?	Come posso giungere a...?
Where is the ...?	Dove si trova...?
Where is the church?	Dove si trova la chiesa?
The museum is next to the shopping center	Il museo si trova vicino al centro commerciale.
The drugstore is in front of the building	La farmacia è di fronte al palazzo
The supermarket is near the park	Il supermercato si trova vicino al parco.

22. The Ordinal Numbers
/ I numeri ordinali

First	**Primo**
Second	**Secondo**
Third	**Terzo**
Fourth	**Quarto**
Fifth	**Quinto**
Sixth	**Sesto**
Seventh	**Settimo**
Eighth	**Ottavo**
Ninth	**Nono**
Tenth	**Decimo**
Eleventh	**Undicesimo**
Twelfth	**Dodicesimo**
Twentieth	**Ventesimo**
Thirtieth	**Trentesimo**
The first building	**Il primo palazzo**
The second floor	**Il secondo piano**

23. Countries, Nationalities, and Languages / Paesi, nazionalità e lingue

Brazil (Country)	**Il brasile**
Brazilian (Nationality)	**Brasiliano/brasiliana**
Portuguese (Language)	**Portoghese(lingua)**
Colombia	**La colombia**
Colombian	**Colombiano**
Spanish	**Lo spagnolo**
China	**La cina**
Chinese	**Il cinese**
Chinese	**Il cinese/la cinese**
England	**L'inghilterra**
English	**Inglese**
English	**L'inglese**
France	**La francia**
French	**Il francese/la francese**
French	**Il francese**
Germany	**La germania**
German	**Tedesco/tedesca**
German	**Il tedesco**
Italy	**L'italia**

23. Countries, Nationalities, and Languages / **Paesi, nazionalità e lingue**

Italian	**Italiano/italiana**
Italian	**L'italiano**
Japan	**Il giappone**
Japanese	**Il giapponese/la giapponese**
Japanese	**Il giapponese**
Mexico	**Il messico**
Mexican	**Messicano/messicana**
Spanish	**Lo spagnolo**
Spain	**La spagna**
Spanish	**Lo spagnolo/la spagnola**
Spanish	**Lo spagnolo**
United States of America (U.S.A.)	**Gli stati uniti d'america (u.S.A.)**
American	**L'americano/l'americana**
English	**L'inglese**
Where are you from?	**Di dov'è?**
I am from Brazil	**Sono del brasile**
I am Brazilian	**Io sono brasiliano**
I speak Portuguese	**Parlo il portoghese**
I am not from Italy	**Non sono dell'italia**

24. Indefinite Pronouns / Pronomi indefiniti

Anybody	**Qualcuno (interrogativo), nessuno (negativo)**
Anything	**Qualcosa (interrogativo), niente (negativo)**
Nobody	**Nessuno**
Nothing	**Niente**
Somebody	**Qualcuno (affirmativo)**
Something	**Qualcosa (affirmativo)**
Everybody	**Tutti**
Everything	**Tutto**
Is anybody home?	**C'è qalcuno a casa?**
I don't want anything	**Non voglio niente**
Nothing happened	**Non è successo niente**
Somebody is in the living room	**C'è qualcuno nella sala**
Everything is ready	**Tutto è pronto**

25. The Emotions
/ Le emozioni

Angry	**Arrabiato**
Bored	**Noioso**
Confident	**Sicuro di se stesso**
Confused	**Confuso**
Embarrassed	**Imbarazzato**
Excited	**Entusiasmato**
Happy	**Contento**
Nervous	**Nervoso**
Proud	**Orgoglioso**
Sad	**Triste**
Scared	**Spaventato**
Shy	**Timido**
Surprised	**Sorpreso**
Worried	**Preoccupato**
I am happy	**Sono contento/felice**
He is sad	**Lui è triste**
They are surprised	**Loro sono sorpresi**
Are you excited?	**Sei entusiasmato?**
I am not bored	**Non sono annoiato**
She is not nervous	**Lei non è nervosa**
Everybody is confident	**Tutti sono sicuri di se stessi**

26. Adverbs / Avverbi

A few	**Qualche**
A little	**Poco**
A lot	**Molto**
After	**Dopo**
Again	**Ancora / di nuovo**
Ago	**Prima**
Also	**Anche**
Always	**Sempre**
Before	**Prima**
Enough	**Sufficentemente**
Everyday	**Ogni giorno**
Exactly	**Esattamente**
Finally	**Finalmente**
First	**Al primo posto**
Here	**Qui**
Late	**Tardi**
Later	**Più tardi**
Never	**Mai**
Next	**Prossimo**
Now	**Adesso**

26. Adverbs
/ Avverbi

Often	**Spesso**
Once	**Una volta**
Only	**Solo**
Outside	**Fuori**
Really	**Davvero**
Right here	**Proprio qui**
Right now	**Proprio adesso/subito**
Since	**Da/da allora**
Slowly	**Lentamente**
Sometimes	**Qualche volta**
Soon	**Presto**
Still	**Ancora**
Then	**Dopo**
There	**Là**
Today	**Oggi**
Tomorrow	**Domani**
Tonight	**Stasera**
Too	**Anche**
Usually	**Di solito**

27. Auxiliary Verbs
/ Verbi ausiliari

English	Italian
Can	**Potere**
Could	**Potrebbe**
Did	**(Ausiliare del pasato)**
Do	**(Ausiliare del presente)**
Does	**(Ausiliare del presente)**
Have to	**Dovere**
May	**Potere**
Must	**Dovere**
Should	**Dovere**
Will	**(Ausiliari del futuro)**
Would	**(Ausiliari condizional)**
Can you go to the movies?	**Puoi venire a cinema?**
Could I have change?	**Potrebbe darmi cambio?**
Did you work at the drugstore?	**Hai lavorato in farmacia?**
I did not (didn't) work at the drugstore	**Non ho lavorato in farmacia**
Do you work at the drugstore?	**Lavori in farmacia?**
I do not (don't) work at the drugstore	**Non lavoro in farmacia**
Does he read the newspaper?	**Lui leggi il giornalo?**
He does not (doesn't) read the newspaper	**Lui non leggi il giornalo**
I have to do my homework	**Devo fare il compito**
May I help you?	**Posso aiutarla?**
You must turn left now	**Devi girare a sinistra**
You should go to the doctor	**Dovresti andare dal medico**
I will work tomorrow	**Lavoro domani**
I would like a glass of wine	**Vorrei un bicchiere di vino**

28. Expressions
/ Espressioni

All right	**Va bene**
Come in	**S' accomodi**
Come here, please	**Venga qui, per favore**
Don't worry!	**Non ti preoccupare**
For example	**Ad esempio**
Good luck!	**Buona fortuna!**
Great idea!	**Ottima idea!**
Have a nice day!	**Buona giornata!**
Help yourself!	**Prego,serviti, pure!**
Here you are	**Prego!**
Hurry up!	**Fai presto!**
I agree	**Sono d'accordo**
I disagree	**Non sono d'accordo**
I don't care	**Non m'interessa**
I don't know	**Non so.**
I'm coming!	**Vengo**
I'm afraid...	**Temo che....**
It's a deal!	**Va bene! D'accordo!**
Keep well!	**Stammi bene!**
Let me think	**Lasciami pensare**
Let's go!	**Andiamo!**
Right now	**Subito**
Sounds good!	**Che bello!**
Sure	**Certo**
Take a seat	**Siediti / si sieda**
Take care!	**Riguardati!**

29. The Family / La famiglia

English	Italian
Father	**Il padre**
Mother	**La madre**
Son	**Il figlio**
Daughter	**La figlia**
Brother	**Il fratello**
Sister	**La sorella**
Grandfather	**Il nonno**
Grandmother	**La nonna**
Uncle	**Lo zio**
Aunt	**La zia**
Cousin	**Il cugino / lacugina**
Nephew	**Il nipote**
Niece	**La nipote**
Husband	**Il marito**
Wife	**La moglie**
Boyfriend	**Il fidanzato / il ragazzo**
Girlfriend	**La fidanzata**
In-laws	**I suoceri**
Father in-law	**Il suocero**
Mother in-law	**La suocera**
Brother in-law	**Il cognato**
Sister in-law	**La cognata**
Step father	**Il patrigno**
Step mother	**La matrigna**
Step brother	**Il fratellastro**
Step sister	**La sorellastra**
Who is he?	**Chi è lui?**
He is my brother	**Questo è mio fratello**

30. The House
/ La casa

Living room	Il soggiorno
Door	La porta
Window	La finestra
Sofa	Il divano
Lamp	La lampada
Dining room	La sala da pranzo
Table	La tavola
Chair	La sedia
Kitchen	La cucina
Stove	La stufa
Oven	Il forno
Fridge	Il frigorifero
Microwave	Il microonde
Bedroom	La camera da letto
Bed	Il letto
Nightstand	Il comodino
Vanity	Il tavolino da toilette
Chest of drawers	Il comò
Closet	Il ripostiglio
Bathroom	La camera da bagno
Mirror	Lo specchio
Sink	Il lavandino
Toilet	La toilette
Bathtub	La vasca
Laundry room	La lavanderia
Driveway	Il parcheggio
Where is the living room?	Dove si trova il soggiorno?
The door is big	La porta è grande.
The stove is small	La stufa è piccola
The kitchen is beautiful	La cucina è bella

31. The City
/ La città

English	Italian
Block	**Il quartiere**
Building	**Il palazzo**
Church	**La chiesa**
Movie theater	**Il cinema**
Museum	**Il museo**
Park	**Il parco**
Drugstore	**La farmacia**
Restaurant	**Il ristorante**
Shopping center	**Il centro commerciale**
Store	**Il negozio**
Street	**La strada**
Supermarket	**Il supermercato**

32. At the Supermarket
/ Al supermercato

The food	**Gli alimentari**
The fruits	**La frutta**
Apple	**La mela**
Banana	**La banana**
Cherry	**La cigliegia**
Grapes	**L'uva**
Orange	**L'arancia**
Strawberry	**La fragola**
The vegetables	**I legumi**
Beans	**I fagioli**
Carrot	**La carota**
Cauliflower	**Il cavolfiore**
Lettuce	**La lattuga**
Onion	**La cipolla**
Pepper	**Il peperone**
Potato	**La patata**
Tomato	**Il pomodoro**
The meats	**La carne**
Beef	**La carne di manzo**
Chicken	**La carne di pollo**
Turkey	**Il tacchino**
Ham	**Il prosciutto**
Pork	**La carne di maiale**
The dairy products	**Latticini**
Butter	**Il burro**
Cheese	**Il formaggio**
Milk	**Il latte**

32. At the Supermarket / Al supermercato

Yogurt	**Lo yogurt**
Jam	**La marmellata**
Bread	**Il pane**
Eggs	**Le uova**
Fish	**Il pesce**
Seafood	**I frutti di mare**
Can	**Le lattine**
Cart	**Il carrello**
Bag	**La borsa**
Basket	**La cesta**
Bottle	**La bottiglia**
Cash register	**La cassa**
Cashier	**Il cassiere/la cassiera**
Customer service	**Servizio clienti**
Groceries	**Le compere**
How many...?	**Quanto ....?**
How many oranges do you buy?	**Quante arance compra?**
How much does it cost?	**Quanto costa?/Quanto costano?**
How much do the bananas cost?	**Quanto costano le banane?**
I want...	**Voglio....**
I want to buy a bottle of milk	**Voglio comprare una bottiglia di latte**
I would like...	**Vorrei...**
I would like a bag of tomatoes	**Vorrei una busta di pomodori....**
Where is the lettuce?	**Dove sono le lattughe?**
It's on aisle one	**Sono nella sezione uno**
Where are the cans of vegetables?	**Dove sono le lattine di legumi?**
They are on aisle five	**Sono nella sezioe numero cinque**

33. At the Restaurant
/ Nel ristorante

Waiter / waitress	**Il cameriere/la cameriera**
Breakfast	**La colazione**
Lunch	**Il pranzo**
Dinner	**La cena**
To eat	**Mangiare**
To drink	**Bere**
To eat breakfast	**Fare colazione**
The menu	**Il menù**
Appetizer	**Il antipasto**
Salad	**L'insalata**
Soup	**La minestra**
Main course	**Il piatto principale**
Pasta	**La pasta**
Rice	**Il riso**
French fries	**Le patate fritte**
Mashed potatoes	**Il purea di patate**
Baked potatoes	**Le patate al forno**
Barbecue	**Il barbecue**
Fried chicken	**Pollo fritto**
Steak	**La bistecca**

33. At the Restaurant
/ Nel ristorante

Dessert	**Il dessert**
Beverages	**Le bevande**
Coffee	**Il caffé**
Tea	**Il té**
Soda	**La bevanda gasata**
Lemonade	**La limonata**
Orange juice	**La spremuta d'arancia**
Alcoholic drinks	**Le bibite alcoliche**
Beer	**La birra**
Wine	**Il vino**
Check	**Il conto**
Tip	**La mancia**
How may I help you?	**Che cosa desidera?**
What would you like to order?	**Che cosa desidera ordinare?**
May I have the menu, please?	**Potrebbe darmi il menù, per favore?**
Could I get more water, please?	**Potrebbe portarmi un po piú d'acqua, per favore?**
My order is wrong	**Non ho ordinato questo**
The service here is wonderful!	**Qui il servizio è eccellente**
The food is delicious!	**Il cibo e delizioso!**
The check, please	**Il conto, per favore**
The tip is included	**La mancia è compresa**

34. The Office
/ L'ufficio

Book	**Il libro**
Calculator	**La calcolatrice**
Computer	**Il computer**
Desk	**La scrivania**
Fax machine	**Il fax**
File	**Il documento**
File cabinet	**L'armadietto dei documenti**
Folder	**La cartelletta**
Keyboard	**La tastiera**
Monitor	**Lo schermo**
Mouse	**Il mouse**
Notebook	**L'agenda**
Pad	**Il blocchetto**
Paper	**La carta**
Pen	**La penna**
Printer	**La stampante**
Ruler	**Il righelo**
Scissors	**Le forbici**
Screen	**Lo schermo**
Stapler	**La graffettatrice**
Telephone	**Il telefono**
My computer is broken	**Il mio computer non funziona**
There is no paper in the printer	**Non c'è carta nella stampante**
We need to buy more folders	**Dobbiamo comprare altre cartelle**
We don't have a copy machine	**Non abbiamo una fotocopiatrice**

35. Jobs and Positions / Posti di lavoro e finzioni

Accountant	**Il ragioniere**
Architect	**L'architetto**
Artist	**L'attore**
Chef	**Il capo cuoco**
Clerk	**L'impiegato/l'impiegata**
Cook	**Il cuoco/la cuoca**
Doctor	**Il dottore**
Engineer	**L'ingegnere**
Gardener	**Il giardiniere**
Graphic designer	**Designer graffico**
Lawyer	**L'avvocato**
Nurse	**L'infermiera**
Physician	**Il medico**
Salesperson	**Il commesso/la commessa**
Secretary	**La segretaria**
Security guard	**Il agente di sicurezza**
Taxi driver	**Autista di taxi**
Teacher	**L'insegnante**
Technician	**Il tecnico**
Tourist guide	**La guida**
Travel agent	**Agente turistico**

36. Job Interview
/ L' Intervista di lavoro

Apply for a job	**Fare domanda di lavoro**
Duty	**La funzione**
Experience	**L'esperienza**
Last name	**Cognome**
First name	**Nome**
Full time job	**Lavoro a tempo pieno**
Part time job	**Lavoro a tempo parziale**
Résumé	**Curriculum vitae**
Skill	**Le abilità**
Work	**Lavorare/il lavoro**

37. The Transportation
/ Mezzi di trasporto

Airplane	**L'aereo**
Bicycle	**La bicicletta**
Bus	**L'autobus**
Car	**La macchina**
Helicopter	**L'elicottero**
Metro	**La metropolitana**
Motorcycle	**La motocicletta**
Train	**Il treno**
Truck	**L'autocarro**

38. The Traffic
/ Il Traffico

Bus stop	**La fermata dell'autobus**
Crosswalk	**Le striscie pedonale**
Freeway, highway	**L'autostrada**
Gas station	**Il distributore di benzina**
Intersection	**L'incrocio**
Lane	**La corsia**
No outlet	**Vicolo ceco**
One way	**A senso unico**
Pedestrian	**Il pedone**
Speed	**La velocità**
Stop sign	**Il segnale "stop"**
To get in	**Salire/entrare**
To get off	**Scendere/uscire**
Toll	**Pagare l'autostrada**
Traffic light	**Il semaforo**
Train station	**La stazione del treno**
Two way	**A due sensi**
U-turn	**Inversione a u**
Yield	**Precedenza**
I get in the car	**Salire in macchina**
I get off the car	**Scendere dalla macchina**
We wait for the train	**Aspettiamo il treno**

39. The Car
/ La macchina

Accelerator	**L'acceleratore**
Battery	**La batteria**
Hood	**Il cofano**
Brake	**Il freno**
Clutch	**La frizione**
Engine	**Il motore**
Fender	**Il paraurto**
Gear box	**La scatola del cambio**
Headlight	**Le luci**
Rear view mirror	**Lo spechietto retrovisore**
Make	**La marca**
Model	**Il modello**
Radiator	**Il radiatore**
Steering wheel	**Il volante**
Seat	**Il sedile**
Tire	**Il pneumatico**
Trunk	**Il baule**
Wheel	**La ruota**
Windshield	**Parabrezza**
Windshield wipers	**I tergicristalli**
The car is broken	**La macchina ha subito un gusto**
I have a flat tire	**Ho la ruota bucata**
I need a new battery	**Ho bisogno di una nuova batteria**
What year is the car?	**Che anno è prodotta la macchina"**
What make is the car?	**Di quale marca è la macchina?**
What model is the car?	**Di che modello è la macchina?**
How many miles does the car have?	**Quante miglia ha la macchina?**

40. Phone Conversations
/ Conversazioni telefoniche

English	Italian
Call	Telefonare / chiamare
Dial	Fare il numero
Directory	L'elenco telefonico
Directory Assistance	L'informazione
Extension	Il numero interno
Hold on, please	Stia in linea, prego / un attimo, per favore
I'd like to speak to...	Vorrei parlare con...
I'll put you through	Le passo.....
I'll transfer your call	Passare la telefonata
I'm calling about ...	Chiamo per....
Just a minute	Aspetti un attimo
Leave a message	Lasciare un messaggio
Let me see...	Mi lasci vedere....
Phone	Chiamare
Phone number	Numero telefonico
Ring	Squillo
Speak	Parlare
Speaking	Sono io
Take a message	Prendere un messaggio
Talk	Parlare
This is...	Parla / chiama....
Who's calling?	Chi parla?

41. At the Post Office
/ Nell'Ufficio postale

Air mail	**La posta aerea**
Counter	**Lo sportello**
Envelope	**La busta**
Letter	**La lettera**
Mail	**La corrispondenza/la posta**
Parcel	**Il pacco**
Postcard	**La cartolina**
Postman, mailman	**Il postino**
Stamp	**Francobollo**
To send	**Inviare**
To deliver	**Consegnare**
Delivery	**La consegna**
To pick up	**Ritirare**
Address	**Indirizzo**
I want to send a letter	**Voglio inviare una lettera**
I would like to pick up a parcel	**Vorrei ritirare un pacco**
How much do the stamps cost?	**Quanto costano i francobolli?**
Do you sell postcards?	**Vendete cartoline?**

42. At the Bank
/ Alla banca

English	Italian
Account	**Conto**
ATM	**Bancomat**
Bank statement	**Estratto conto**
Bank teller	**Cassiere/cassiera**
Cash	**Soldi in contanti**
Checkbook	**Il libretto degli assegni**
Checking account	**Il conto corrente**
Credit card	**La carta di credito**
Debit card	**La carta del bancomat**
Deposit slip	**La ricevuta di deposito**
Savings account	**Il deposito di risparmio**
To deposit	**Depositare**
To save	**Risparmiare**
To transfer	**Trasferire**
To withdraw	**Prelevare**
Transactions	**La transazione**
Withdrawal slip	**Lo scontrino di prolievo**
I want to make a deposit	**Vorrei fare un deposito**
Do you have a savings account?	**Lei ha un conto di risparmio?**
I have a checking account	**Ho un conto corrente**
What is your credit card number?	**Quale è il numero della sua carta di credito?**
I don't have an ATM card	**Non ho una carta per bancomat**
Where are the deposit slips?	**Dove sono i moduli per il versamento?**

43. At the Airport
/ All'aeroporto

Arrival	**L'arrivo**
Concourse	**Il corridoio**
Customs	**La dogana**
Departure	**La partenza**
Destination	**La destinazione**
Entrance	**L'entrata**
Exit	**L'uscita**
First class	**La prima classe**
Flight	**Il volo**
Gate	**Il terminale**
Immigrations office	**L'ufficio immigrazioni**
Luggage	**Il bagaglio**
Passport	**Il passaporti**
Restrooms	**Le toilette**
Suitcase	**La valigia**
To arrive	**Arrivare**
To depart	**Partire**
To travel	**Viaggiare**
Trip	**Il viaggio**
Where are you traveling?	**Dove va?**
May I have your ticket, please?	**Posso vedere il suo biglietto, per favore?**
I need you passport, please	**Mi fa vedere il suo passaporto, per favore?**
My flight number is ...	**Il numero del mio volo è**
Where is gate number ...?	**Dov'è il numero del terminale**
The flight is delayed	**L'aereo arriva in ritardo**
The flight is on time	**L'aereo arriva in orario**

44. At the Hotel
/ All'albergo

Double room	**Una camera doppia**
Single room	**Una camera singola**
Bell desk	**La reception**
Bellman	**Il facchino**
Elevator	**L'ascensore**
Reception	**La ricezione**
Receptionist	**Il ricezionista/la ricezionista**
Reservation	**La prenotazione**
Stairway	**Le scale**
Swimming pool	**La piscina**
Tours desk	**L'agenzia turistica**
Valet parking	**Il servizio di parcheggio**
To check-in	**La registrazione**
To check-out	**Pagare il conto dell'albergo**
I would like to make a reservation	**Vorrei fare una prenotazione**
I want a single room	**Voglio una camera singola**
I would like to check-in	**Vorrei registrarmi**

45. The Clothes
/ L'abbigliamento

Bathing suit	**Il costume da bagno**
Belt	**La cintura**
Blouse	**La camicetta**
Coat	**Il cappotto**
Dress	**Il vestito**
Gloves	**I guanti**
Hat	**Il cappello**
Jacket	**La giacca**
Pants	**I pantaloni**
Purse	**La borsa**
Scarf	**La sciarpa**
Shirt	**La camicia**
Shoes	**Le scarpe**
Shorts	**I pantaloncini corti**
Skirt	**La gonna**
Socks	**Le calze**
Suit	**Il completo**
Suitcase	**La valigia**
The size	**La taglia**
Small	**Piccolo**
Medium	**Medio**
Large	**Grande**
Big sizes	**Le taglie grandi**

46. At the Shopping Center
/ Al centro commerciale

Department store	**Grande magazzino**
Ladies	**Donne**
Men	**Uomini**
Juniors	**Giovani**
Kids	**Bambini**
Ladies' department	**Reparto donne**
Jewelry	**La gioilleria**
Fitting room	**Il camerino**
Elevator	**L'ascensore**
Escalator	**La scala mobile**
How may I help you?	**Posso aiutarla?**
I'm looking for ...	**Sto cercando....**
I'm just looking	**Sto guardando..**
Where is the fitting room?	**Dov'è il camerino?**
It fits well	**Mi va bene**
It doesn't fit well	**Non mi va bene**
May I pay here?	**Posso pagare qui?**
I want to exchange this	**Voglio cambiare questo**
I want to return this	**Vorrei restituire questo**
I like ...	**Mi piace/mi piacciono**
I like this blouse	**Questa camicetta mi piace**
I don't like ...	**Non mi piace/non mi piacciono**
I don't like these pants	**Questi pantaloni non mi piacciono**

47. At the Drugstore
/ Alla farmacia

English	Italian
Antiseptic	**Il disinfettante**
Adhesive bandage	**Il cerotto**
Antibiotic	**L'antibiotico**
Aspirin	**L'aspirina**
Bandage	**La fascia**
Cold medicine	**Medicinale per raffreddore**
Cough syrup	**Sciroppo per tosse**
Medication	**I medicinali**
Ointment	**La pomata**
OTC (Over The Counter) medication	**Medicinali da banco**
Painkiller	**Analgetico**
Pills	**Le pastiglie**
Prescription	**La ricetta medica**
Tablets	**Le pillole**
Thermometer	**Il termometro**
Cotton	**Il cotone**

48. The Parts of the Body
/ Le parti del corpo umano

Ankle	**La caviglia**
Arm	**La mano**
Back	**La schiena**
Buttock	**Il sedere**
Calf	**Il polpaccio**
Chest	**Il petto**
Elbow	**Il gomito**
Feet	**I piedi**
Finger	**Il dito**
Foot	**Il piede**
Forearm	**Il braccio**
Hand	**La mano**
Head	**La testa**
Hip	**Il fianco**
Knee	**Il ginocchio**
Leg	**La gamba**
Neck	**Il collo**
Shoulder	**La spalla**
Stomach	**Lo stomaco**
Thigh	**La coscia**
Toe	**Il dito del piede**
Waist	**La vita**
Wrist	**Il polso**

49. Health Problems
/ Problemi di salute

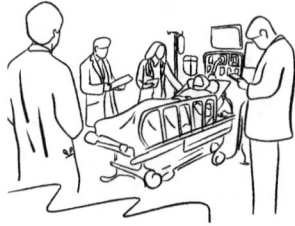

Backache	**Dolore alla schiena**
Cold	**Il raffreddore**
Fever	**La febbre**
Hurt	**Fa male**
Indigestion	**Cattiva digestione**
Injury	**La ferita**
Pain	**Il dolore**
Pulse	**Il polso**
Sick	**Malato**
Sneeze	**Lo starnuto**
Sore throat	**Mal di gola**
Toothache	**Mal di denti**
I have a headache	**Ho mal di testa**
I have a stomachache	**Ho mal di stomaco**
I have pain in my knee	**Mi fa male il ginocchio**
I hurt my hand	**Mi sono fatto male alla mano**
I've got a cold	**Ho preso un raffreddore**
My foot hurts	**Mi fa male la gamba**

50. The Animals
/ Gli animali

English	Italian
Bear	**L'orso**
Bird	**L'uccello**
Cat	**Il gatto**
Chicken	**Il pollo**
Cow	**La mucca**
Dog	**Il cane**
Duck	**L'anatra**
Elephant	**L'elefante**
Fish	**Il pesce**
Horse	**Il cavallo**
Lizard	**La lucertola**
Lion	**Il leone**
Monkey	**La scimmia**
Mouse	**Il topolino**
Rat	**Il topo**
Tiger	**La tigre**

EXERCISE!

Write the Italian translation.

Keep practicing at:
QuickLanguages.com

1. Greetings
/ Saluti

Hi! / Hello!	Ciao / Salve!
Good morning	
Good afternoon	
Good evening / Good night	
How are you doing?	
Fine	
Very well	
Thank you / Thanks	
Thank you very much	
You're welcome	
Fine, thank you	
And you?	
See you	
See you later	
See you tomorrow	
Goodbye	
Bye	

2. Introductions and Courtesy Expressions / **Presentazione ed espressioni di cortesia**

What is your name?

Come si chiama?

My name is ...

Who are you?

I am ...

Who is he / she?

He is ... / She is ...

Nice to meet you / Pleased to meet you

Nice to meet you, too

It's my pleasure

Excuse me

Please

One moment, please

Welcome

Go ahead

Can you repeat, please?

I don't understand

I understand a little

Can you speak more slowly, please?

Do you speak Spanish?

How do you say hello in Spanish?

What does it mean?

I speak Spanish a little

3. Ways to Address a Person / **Forme per rivolgersi ad una persona**

Madam / Ma'am	Signora
Miss	
Ms.	
Mr.	
Mrs.	
Sir	
Dr.	

4. The Articles / **L'articolo determinativo e indeterminativo**

The	il, lo, l' / la, l' / i, gli / le
The car	
The cars	
The house	
The houses	
A	
A car	
A house	
An	
An elephant	
An apple	
Some	
Some cars	
Some houses	

5. The Subject Pronouns
/ Pronomi personali

I	Io
You	
He	
She	
It	
We	
You	
They	

6. The Possessive Adjectives
/ Gli Aggettivi possessivi

My	Mio / a
Your	
His	
Her	
Its	
Our	
Your	
Their	
My car	
Your book	
His TV	
Our house	

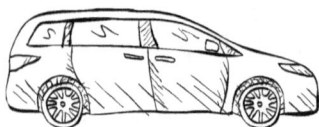

7. The Demonstrative Adjectives / Gli Aggettivi dimostrativi

This	Questo / questa
This book	
This shirt	
These	
These books	
These shirts	
That	
That table	
That car	
Those	
Those tables	
Those cars	

8. The Possessive Pronouns / I pronomi possessivi

Mine	Mio, mia miei, mie
Yours	
His	
Hers	
Its	
Ours	
Yours	
Theirs	
The car is mine	
The book is yours	
That TV is his	
This house is ours	

9. The Cardinal Numbers
/ I numeri cardinali

0 / Zero	Zero
1 / One	
2 / Two	
3 / Three	
4 / Four	
5 / Five	
6 / Six	
7 / Seven	
8 / Eight	
9 / Nine	
10 / Ten	
11 / Eleven	
12 / Twelve	
13 / Thirteen	
14 / Fourteen	
15 / Fifteen	
16 / Sixteen	
17 / Seventeen	
18 / Eighteen	
19 / Nineteen	
20 / Twenty	
21 / Twenty-one	
30 / Thirty	
40 / Forty	
50 / Fifty	
60 / Sixty	

1. 2. 3. 4.
5. 6. 7. 8.
9. 0.

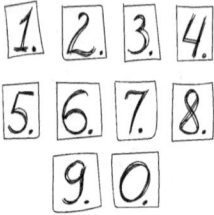

9. The Cardinal Numbers
/ I numeri cardinali

70 / Seventy	*Settanta*
80 / Eighty	
90 /Ninety	
100 / One hundred	
101 / One hundred and one	
200 / Two hundred	
300 / Three hundred	
400 / Four hundred	
500 / Five hundred	
600 / Six hundred	
700 / Seven hundred	
800 / Eight hundred	
900 /Nine hundred	
1,000 / One thousand	
10,000 / Ten thousand	
100,000 / One hundred thousand	
1,000,000 / One million	
1,000,000,000 / One billion	
Forty-five (45)	
One hundred and twenty-eight (128)	
One thousand nine hundred and sixty-three (1,963)	
Six thousand and thirty-seven (6,037)	
Eleven thousand (11,000)	
Two hundred and seventy-nine thousand (279,000)	
Two million (2,000,000)	

10. The Time
/ L'ora

The clock	*l'orologio da muro*
The watch	
What time is it?	
It is ...	
It is one o'clock (1:00)	
It is two o'clock (2:00)	
It is three fifteen / It is a quarter past three (3:15)	
It is four thirty / It is half past four (4:30)	
It is five forty-five / It is a quarter to six (5:45)	
It is six fifty / It is ten to seven (6:50)	
It is noon (12:00 P. M.)	
It is midnight (12:00 A. M.)	
In the morning	
In the afternoon	
In the evening	
At night	
At what time is ...?	
At what time is the concert?	
At ...	
At 7:10 P.M. (seven ten in the evening)	

11. The Days of the Week
/ I giorni della settimana

Monday	Lunedi
Tuesday	
Wednesday	
Thursday	
Friday	
Saturday	
Sunday	
What day is today?	

12. The Months of the Year
/ I mesi dell'anno

January	Gennaio
February	
March	
April	
May	
June	
July	
August	
September	
October	
November	
December	
What is today's date?	

13. The Weather
/ Il Tempo

English	Italian
Sunny	Soleggiato
Cloudy	
Rainy	
Humid	
Dry	
Cold	
Warm	
Hot	
Rain	
Snow	
How is the weather today?	
It's nice	
It's sunny	
It's cold in winter	
It's raining	
It's snowing	
I am cold	

14. The Seasons / Le stagioni

Spring	La primavera
Summer	
Fall	
Winter	

15. The Colors / I colori

Yellow	Giallo
Red	
Blue	
Green	
Orange	
Brown	
Pink	
Purple	
Black	
White	
Gray	
Light	
Dark	
Light green	
Orange book	
Brown shoes	
My blouse is white	
What color is...?	
What is your favorite color?	

16. The Parts of the Face
/ Le Parti della Faccia

La guancia

Cheek	
Chin	
Ear	
Eye	
Forehead	
Hair	
Lips	
Mouth	
Nose	
Skin	
Teeth	
Tooth	
Blond / Blonde	
Brown	
Gray	
Red hair	
Long	
Short	
Straight	
Curly	
John is blond	
Karen has long hair	
He has green eyes	
Her eyes are blue	
His eyes are big and brown	

17. Essential Verbs
/ Verbi Essenziali

Be	Essere
Go	
Come	
Have	
Get	
Help	
Love	
Like	
Want	
Buy	
Sell	
Read	
Write	
Drink	
Eat	
Open	
Close	
Look at	
Look for	
Find	
Start	
Stop	
Pull	

17. Essential Verbs
/ Verbi Essenziali

Push — *Spingere*

Send

Receive

Turn on

Turn off

Listen to

Speak

Do

Drive

Feel

Know

Leave

Live

Make

Meet

Need

Pay

Play

Remember

Repeat

Say

Sit

Sleep

17. Essential Verbs / Verbi Essenziali

Study	Studiare
Take	
Think	
Understand	
Wait	
Watch	
There is	
There are	
I am tall	
You are short	
He is thin	
We are big	
They are intelligent	
I am at home	
You are at school	
We are at the store	
I get a prize	
I go to the movies	
I have a nice car	
I listen to the music	
I watch TV.	
I like this book	
There are ten children in the park	

18. Interrogative Words
/ Pronomi interrogativi

How many ...?	Quanti/e...?
How much...?	
How ...?	
What ...?	
When ...?	
Where ...?	
Which ...?	
Who ...?	
Whose ...?	
Whom ...? / To whom ...?	
Why ...?	
Because ...	

19. Linking Words
/ Le congiunzioni

And	E
But	
Or	
Either ... or	
Neither ... nor	
Yes	
No	
So	
While	

20. The Prepositions
/ Le preposizioni

About	Circa
Above	
Across	
At	
Behind	
Below	
Between	
By	
Down	
During	
For	
From	
In	
In front of	
Into	

20. The Prepositions
/ Le preposizioni

Near	Vicino a
Next to	
Of	
On	
Out	
Over	
Per	
Through	
To	
Under	
Up	
With	
Without	
The cat is in the box	
The vase is on the table	
Somebody is at the door	

21. Giving Directions / Dare istruzioni

At the corner	All'angolo
Far	
Near	
Go straight ahead	
Left	
Right	
Turn left	
Turn right	
Go straight one block	
After the traffic light, turn right	
How can I get to ...?	
Where is the ...?	
Where is the church?	
The museum is next to the shopping center	
The drugstore is in front of the building	
The supermarket is near the park	

22. The Ordinal Numbers
/ I numeri ordinali

First	Primo
Second	
Third	
Fourth	
Fifth	
Sixth	
Seventh	
Eighth	
Ninth	
Tenth	
Eleventh	
Twelfth	
Twentieth	
Thirtieth	
The first building	
The second floor	

23. Countries, Nationalities, and Languages / **Paesi, nazionalità e lingue**

Brazil (Country)	Il Brasile
Brazilian (Nationality)	
Portuguese (Language)	
Colombia	
Colombian	
Spanish	
China	
Chinese	
Chinese	
England	
English	
English	
France	
French	
French	
Germany	
German	
German	
Italy	

23. Countries, Nationalities, and Languages / **Paesi, nazionalità e lingue**

Italian	Italiano / italiana
Italian	
Japan	
Japanese	
Japanese	
Mexico	
Mexican	
Spanish	
Spain	
Spanish	
Spanish	
United States of America (U.S.A.)	
American	
English	
Where are you from?	
I am from Brazil	
I am Brazilian	
I speak Portuguese	
I am not from Italy	

24. Indefinite Pronouns / Pronomi indefiniti

Anybody	Qualcuno (interrogativo), nessuno (negativo)
Anything	
Nobody	
Nothing	
Somebody	
Something	
Everybody	
Everything	
Is anybody home?	
I don't want anything	
Nothing happened	
Somebody is in the living room	
Everything is ready	

25. The Emotions
/ Le emozioni

Angry	Arrabiato
Bored	
Confident	
Confused	
Embarrassed	
Excited	
Happy	
Nervous	
Proud	
Sad	
Scared	
Shy	
Surprised	
Worried	
I am happy	
He is sad	
They are surprised	
Are you excited?	
I am not bored	
She is not nervous	
Everybody is confident	

26. Adverbs
/ Avverbi

A few	Qualche
A little	
A lot	
After	
Again	
Ago	
Also	
Always	
Before	
Enough	
Everyday	
Exactly	
Finally	
First	
Here	
Late	
Later	
Never	
Next	
Now	

26. Adverbs
/ Avverbi

Often	Spesso
Once	
Only	
Outside	
Really	
Right here	
Right now	
Since	
Slowly	
Sometimes	
Soon	
Still	
Then	
There	
Today	
Tomorrow	
Tonight	
Too	
Usually	

27. Auxiliary Verbs
/ Verbi ausiliari

Can	*Potere*
Could	
Did	
Do	
Does	
Have to	
May	
Must	
Should	
Will	
Would	
Can you go to the movies?	
Could I have change?	
Did you work at the drugstore?	
I did not (didn't) work at the drugstore	
Do you work at the drugstore?	
I do not (don't) work at the drugstore	
Does he read the newspaper?	
He does not (doesn't) read the newspaper	
I have to do my homework	
May I help you?	
You must turn left now	
You should go to the doctor	
I will work tomorrow	
I would like a glass of wine	

28. Expressions
/ Espressioni

All right	Va bene
Come in	
Come here, please	
Don't worry!	
For example	
Good luck!	
Great idea!	
Have a nice day!	
Help yourself!	
Here you are	
Hurry up!	
I agree	
I disagree	
I don't care	
I don't know	
I'm coming!	
I'm afraid...	
It's a deal!	
Keep well!	
Let me think	
Let's go!	
Right now	
Sounds good!	
Sure	
Take a seat	
Take care!	

29. The Family
/ La famiglia

Father	Il padre
Mother	
Son	
Daughter	
Brother	
Sister	
Grandfather	
Grandmother	
Uncle	
Aunt	
Cousin	
Nephew	
Niece	
Husband	
Wife	
Boyfriend	
Girlfriend	
In-laws	
Father in-law	
Mother in-law	
Brother in-law	
Sister in-law	
Step father	
Step mother	
Step brother	
Step sister	
Who is he?	
He is my brother	

30. The House
/ La casa

Living room	Il soggiorno
Door	
Window	
Sofa	
Lamp	
Dining room	
Table	
Chair	
Kitchen	
Stove	
Oven	
Fridge	
Microwave	
Bedroom	
Bed	
Nightstand	
Vanity	
Chest of drawers	
Closet	
Bathroom	
Mirror	
Sink	
Toilet	
Bathtub	
Laundry room	
Driveway	
Where is the living room?	
The door is big	
The stove is small	
The kitchen is beautiful	

31. The City
/ La città

Block	Il quartiere
Building	
Church	
Movie theater	
Museum	
Park	
Drugstore	
Restaurant	
Shopping center	
Store	
Street	
Supermarket	

32. At the Supermarket
/ Al supermercato

The food	Gli alimentari
The fruits	
Apple	
Banana	
Cherry	
Grapes	
Orange	
Strawberry	
The vegetables	
Beans	
Carrot	
Cauliflower	
Lettuce	
Onion	
Pepper	
Potato	
Tomato	
The meats	
Beef	
Chicken	
Turkey	
Ham	
Pork	
The dairy products	
Butter	
Cheese	
Milk	

32. At the Supermarket / Al supermercato

English	Italian
Yogurt	Lo yogurt
Jam	
Bread	
Eggs	
Fish	
Seafood	
Can	
Cart	
Bag	
Basket	
Bottle	
Cash register	
Cashier	
Customer service	
Groceries	
How many...?	
How many oranges do you buy?	
How much does it cost?	
How much do the bananas cost?	
I want...	
I want to buy a bottle of milk	
I would like...	
I would like a bag of tomatoes	
Where is the lettuce?	
It's on aisle one	
Where are the cans of vegetables?	
They are on aisle five	

33. At the Restaurant
/ Nel ristorante

Waiter / waitress	Il cameriere / la cameriera
Breakfast	
Lunch	
Dinner	
To eat	
To drink	
To eat breakfast	
The menu	
Appetizer	
Salad	
Soup	
Main course	
Pasta	
Rice	
French fries	
Mashed potatoes	
Baked potatoes	
Barbecue	
Fried chicken	
Steak	

33. At the Restaurant
/ Nel ristorante

Dessert	Il dessert
Beverages	
Coffee	
Tea	
Soda	
Lemonade	
Orange juice	
Alcoholic drinks	
Beer	
Wine	
Check	
Tip	
How may I help you?	
What would you like to order?	
May I have the menu, please?	
Could I get more water, please?	
My order is wrong	
The service here is wonderful!	
The food is delicious!	
The check, please	
The tip is included	

34. The Office
/ L'ufficio

Book   Il libro

Calculator

Computer

Desk

Fax machine

File

File cabinet

Folder

Keyboard

Monitor

Mouse

Notebook

Pad

Paper

Pen

Printer

Ruler

Scissors

Screen

Stapler

Telephone

My computer is broken

There is no paper in the printer

We need to buy more folders

We don't have a copy machine

35. Jobs and Positions
/ Posti di lavoro e finzioni

English	Italian
Accountant	Il ragioniere
Architect	
Artist	
Chef	
Clerk	
Cook	
Doctor	
Engineer	
Gardener	
Graphic designer	
Lawyer	
Nurse	
Physician	
Salesperson	
Secretary	
Security guard	
Taxi driver	
Teacher	
Technician	
Tourist guide	
Travel agent	

36. Job Interview
/ L' Intervista di lavoro

Apply for a job	Fare domanda di lavoro
Duty	
Experience	
Last name	
First name	
Full time job	
Part time job	
Résumé	
Skill	
Work	

37. The Transportation
/ Mezzi di trasporto

Airplane	l'aereo
Bicycle	
Bus	
Car	
Helicopter	
Metro	
Motorcycle	
Train	
Truck	

38. The Traffic
/ Il Traffico

Bus stop	La fermata dell'autobus
Crosswalk	
Freeway, highway	
Gas station	
Intersection	
Lane	
No outlet	
One way	
Pedestrian	
Speed	
Stop sign	
To get in	
To get off	
Toll	
Traffic light	
Train station	
Two way	
U-turn	
Yield	
I get in the car	
I get off the car	
We wait for the train	

39. The Car
/ La macchina

Accelerator	*l'acceleratore*
Battery	
Hood	
Brake	
Clutch	
Engine	
Fender	
Gear box	
Headlight	
Rear view mirror	
Make	
Model	
Radiator	
Steering wheel	
Seat	
Tire	
Trunk	
Wheel	
Windshield	
Windshield wipers	
The car is broken	
I have a flat tire	
I need a new battery	
What year is the car?	
What make is the car?	
What model is the car?	
How many miles does the car have?	

40. Phone Conversations
/ Conversazioni telefoniche

English	Italian
Call	Telefonare / chiamare
Dial	
Directory	
Directory Assistance	
Extension	
Hold on, please	
I'd like to speak to...	
I'll put you through	
I'll transfer your call	
I'm calling about ...	
Just a minute	
Leave a message	
Let me see...	
Phone	
Phone number	
Ring	
Speak	
Speaking	
Take a message	
Talk	
This is...	
Who's calling?	

41. At the Post Office
/ Nell'Ufficio postale

Air mail	La posta aerea
Counter	
Envelope	
Letter	
Mail	
Parcel	
Postcard	
Postman, mailman	
Stamp	
To send	
To deliver	
Delivery	
To pick up	
Address	
I want to send a letter	
I would like to pick up a parcel	
How much do the stamps cost?	
Do you sell postcards?	

42. At the Bank / Alla banca

English	Italian
Account	Conto
ATM	
Bank statement	
Bank teller	
Cash	
Checkbook	
Checking account	
Credit card	
Debit card	
Deposit slip	
Savings account	
To deposit	
To save	
To transfer	
To withdraw	
Transactions	
Withdrawal slip	
I want to make a deposit	
Do you have a savings account?	
I have a checking account	
What is your credit card number?	
I don't have an ATM card	
Where are the deposit slips?	

43. At the Airport
/ All'aeroporto

Arrival	L'arrivo
Concourse	
Customs	
Departure	
Destination	
Entrance	
Exit	
First class	
Flight	
Gate	
Immigrations office	
Luggage	
Passport	
Restrooms	
Suitcase	
To arrive	
To depart	
To travel	
Trip	
Where are you traveling?	
May I have your ticket, please?	
I need you passport, please	
My flight number is ...	
Where is gate number ...?	
The flight is delayed	
The flight is on time	

44. At the Hotel
/ All'albergo

English	Italian
Double room	Una camera doppia
Single room	
Bell desk	
Bellman	
Elevator	
Reception	
Receptionist	
Reservation	
Stairway	
Swimming pool	
Tours desk	
Valet parking	
To check-in	
To check-out	
I would like to make a reservation	
I want a single room	
I would like to check-in	

45. The Clothes
/ L'abbigliamento

Bathing suit	Il costume da bagno
Belt	
Blouse	
Coat	
Dress	
Gloves	
Hat	
Jacket	
Pants	
Purse	
Scarf	
Shirt	
Shoes	
Shorts	
Skirt	
Socks	
Suit	
Suitcase	
The size	
Small	
Medium	
Large	
Big sizes	

46. At the Shopping Center / Al centro commerciale

Department store	Grande magazzino
Ladies	
Men	
Juniors	
Kids	
Ladies' department	
Jewelry	
Fitting room	
Elevator	
Escalator	
How may I help you?	
I'm looking for ...	
I'm just looking	
Where is the fitting room?	
It fits well	
It doesn't fit well	
May I pay here?	
I want to exchange this	
I want to return this	
I like ...	
I like this blouse	
I don't like ...	
I don't like these pants	

47. At the Drugstore
/ Alla farmacia

English	Italian
Antiseptic	Il disinfettante
Adhesive bandage	
Antibiotic	
Aspirin	
Bandage	
Cold medicine	
Cough syrup	
Medication	
Ointment	
OTC (Over The Counter) medication	
Painkiller	
Pills	
Prescription	
Tablets	
Thermometer	
Cotton	

48. The Parts of the Body
/ Le parti del corpo umano

English	Italian
Ankle	La caviglia
Arm	
Back	
Buttock	
Calf	
Chest	
Elbow	
Feet	
Finger	
Foot	
Forearm	
Hand	
Head	
Hip	
Knee	
Leg	
Neck	
Shoulder	
Stomach	
Thigh	
Toe	
Waist	
Wrist	

49. Health Problems
/ Problemi di salute

Backache	*Dolore alla schiena*
Cold	
Fever	
Hurt	
Indigestion	
Injury	
Pain	
Pulse	
Sick	
Sneeze	
Sore throat	
Toothache	
I have a headache	
I have a stomachache	
I have pain in my knee	
I hurt my hand	
I've got a cold	
My foot hurts	

50. The Animals
/ Gli animali

Bear	l'orso
Bird	
Cat	
Chicken	
Cow	
Dog	
Duck	
Elephant	
Fish	
Horse	
Lizard	
Lion	
Monkey	
Mouse	
Rat	
Tiger	

EXERCISE!

Write the English translation.

Keep practicing at:
QuickLanguages.com

1. Greetings
/ Saluti

Ciao / salve!	Hi! / Hello!
Buon giorno!	
Buon giorno!	
Buona sera! / Buona notte!	
Come stai?	
Bene	
Molto bene	
Grazie	
Grazie mille	
Prego	
Va bene, grazie	
E tu?	
A presto	
A presto! Ciao!	
A domani	
Arrivederci!	
Ciao!	

2. Introductions and Courtesy Expressions / **Presentazione ed espressioni di cortesia**

Italian	English
Come si chiama?	What is your name?
Mi chiamo...	
Chi è Lei?	
Io sono....	
Chi è Lui?/ Chi è Lei?	
Lui è.../Lei è....	
Piacere di conoscerLa	
Anche per me è un piacere di conoscerLa!	
Il piacere è mio	
La prego di scusarmi	
Per favore/prego	
Un attimo, prego	
Benvenuto!	
Prego, s'accomodi	
Potrebbe ripetere, per favore?	
Non capisco	
Capisco un po'	
Potrebbe parlare più lentamente per favore?	
Parla Spagnolo?	
Come si dice "salve" in Spagnolo?	
Che cosa significa questo?	
Parlo un po' lo Spagnolo.	

3. Ways to Address a Person / **Forme per rivolgersi ad una persona**

Signora	Madam / Ma'am
Signorina	
Sig.na	
Sig	
Sig.ra	
Signore	
Dottore	

4. The Articles / **L'articolo determinativo e indeterminativo**

il, lo, l' / la, l' / I, gli / le	The
la macchina	
le macchine	
la casa	
le case	
Un,uno / una,un'	
una macchina	
una casa	
un' (quando la parola in femminile comincia con una vocale)	
un elefante	
una mela	
dei, delle, degli	
delle macchine	
delle case	

5. The Subject Pronouns
/ Pronomi personali

Io	I
Tu	
Lui	
Lei	
Ø	
Noi	
Voi	
Loro	

6. The Possessive Adjectives
/ Gli Aggettivi possessivi

Mio/a	My
Tuo/a	
Suo/a	
Suo/a	
Suo/a	
Nostro/a	
Vostro/a	
Loro	
La mia macchina	
Il tuo libro	
Il suo televisore	
La nostra casa	

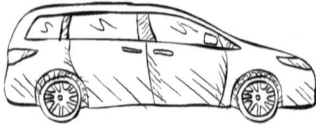

7. The Demonstrative Adjectives / Gli Aggettivi dimostrativi

Questo / questa	This
Questo libro	
Questa camicia	
Questi / queste	
Questi libri	
Queste camicie	
Quel,quello / quella	
Quel tavolo	
Quella macchina	
Quei, quegli / quelle	
Quei tavoli	
Quelle macchine	

8. The Possessive Pronouns / I pronomi possessivi

Mio, mia miei, mie	Mine
Tuo, Tua, tuoi, tue	
Suo, suoi, sue	
Sua, suoi, sue	
Suo, suoi, sue	
Nostro/a, nostri, nostre	
Vostro/a, votri, vostre	
Loro	
La macchina è mia	
Il libro è tuo	
Questo è il suo televisore	
Questa è la nostra casa	

9. The Cardinal Numbers
/ I numeri cardinali

Zero	0 / Zero
Uno	
Due	
Tre	
Quattro	
Cinque	
Sei	
Sette	
Otto	
Nove	
Dieci	
Undici	
Dodici	
Tredici	
Quattordici	
Quindici	
Sedici	
Diciasette	
Diciotto	
Diciannove	
Venti	
Ventuno	
Trenta	
Quaranta	
Cinquanta	
Sessanta	

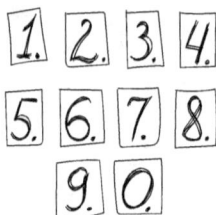

9. The Cardinal Numbers / I numeri cardinali

Settanta	70 / Seventy
Ottanta	
Novanta	
Cento	
Centuno	
Duecento	
Trecento	
Quattrocento	
Cinquecento	
Seicento	
Settecento	
Ottocento	
Novecento	
Mille	
Diecimila	
Centomila	
Un milione	
Un miliardo	
Quarantacinque	
Centoventotto	
Millenovecentosessantatre	
Seimilatrentasette	
Undicimila	
Duecentosettantanovemila	
Duemilioni	

10. The Time
/ L'ora

l'orologio da muro	The clock
l'orologio da polso	
Che ore sono?	
Sono le...	
E' l'una	
Sono le due	
Sono le tre e un quarto	
Sono le quattro e mezza	
Sono le cinque e quarantacinque/sono le sei meno quindici	
Sono le sei e cinquanta/sono le sette meno dieci	
E' mezzoggiorno	
E' mezzanotte	
La mattina	
Il pomeriggio	
La notte	
Durante la notte	
A che ora è.../	
A che ora comincia il concerto?	
Alle....	
Alle diciannove e dieci	

11. The Days of the Week / I giorni della settimana

Lunedì	Monday
Martedì	
Mercoledì	
Giovedì	
Venerdì	
Sabato	
Domenica	
Che giorno è oggi?	

12. The Months of the Year / I mesi dell'anno

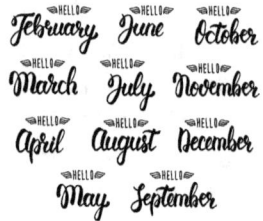

Gennaio	January
Febbraio	
Marzo	
Aprile	
Maggio	
Giugno	
Luglio	
Agosto	
Settembre	
Ottobre	
Novembre	
Dicembre	
Che data è oggi?	

13. The Weather
/ Il Tempo

Soleggiato	Sunny
Nuvoloso	
Piovoso	
Umido	
Secco	
Freddo	
Caldo	
Molto caldo	
La pioggia	
La neve	
Che tempo fa oggi?	
Fa bel tempo	
E' soleggiato	
D'inverno fa freddo	
Piove	
Nevica	
Ho freddo	

14. The Seasons / Le stagioni

La primavera	Spring
L'estate	
L'autunno	
L'inverno	

15. The Colors / I colori

Giallo	Yellow
Rosso	
Blu	
Verde	
Arancione	
Marrone	
Rosa	
Lilla	
Nero	
Bianco	
Grigio	
Chiaro	
Scuro	
Verde chiaro	
Un libro arancione	
Delle scarpe marroni	
La mia camicetta è bianca	
Di che colore è	
Qual'è il tuo colore preferito?	

16. The Parts of the Face
/ Le Parti della Faccia

La guancia	Cheek
Il mento	
L'orecchio	
L'occhio	
La fronte	
I capelli	
Le labbra	
La bocca	
Il naso	
La pelle	
I denti	
Il dente	
Biondo/bionda	
Castano	
Biancho	
Capelli rossi	
Lunghi	
Corti	
Lisci	
Ricci	
Giovanni è biondo	
Karen ha i capelli lunghi	
Lui ha gli occhi verdi	
Lei ha gli occhi azzurri	
Lui ha gli occhi grandi e marroni	

17. Essential Verbs
/ Verbi Essenziali

Essere	Be
Andare	
Venire	
Avere	
Prendere	
Aiutare	
Amare	
Piacere	
Volere	
Comprare	
Vendere	
Leggere	
Scrivere	
Bere	
Mangiare	
Aprire	
Chiudere	
Guardare	
Cercare	
Trovare	
Cominciare	
Fermarsi	
Tirare	

17. Essential Verbs
/ Verbi Essenziali

Spingere   Push

Inviare

Ricevere

Accendere

Speanere

Ascoltare

Parlare

Fare

Guidare

Sentire

Sapere

Rimanere / uscire

Vivere

Preparare

Conoscere / Incontrare

Avere bisogno

Pagare

Giocare

Ricordare

Ripetere

Dire

Sedersi

Dormire

17. Essential Verbs / Verbi Essenziali

Studiare	*Study*
Prendere	
Pensare	
Capire	
Aspettare	
Guardare / osservare	
C'è	
Ci sono	
Sono alto	
Sono basso	
Lui è magro	
Noi siamo grandi	
Loro sono intelligenti	
Sono a casa	
Loro sono a scuola	
Noi siamo al negozio	
Ho preso un premio	
Vado al cinema	
Ho un bella macchina	
Ascolto la musica	
Guardo la televisione	
Questo libro mi piace	
Nel parco ci sono dieci bambini	

18. Interrogative Words
/ Pronomi interrogativi

Quanti/e...?	How many ...?
Quanto/a...?	
Come...?	
Che cosa...?	
Quando...?	
Dove...?	
Quale...?	
Chi...?	
Di chi...?	
A chi...? Per chi...?	
Perchè...?	
Perchè...	

19. Linking Words
/ Le congiunzioni

E	And
Ma	
O	
O...o	
Nè...nè	
Si	
No	
Allora	
Mentre	

20. The Prepositions
/ Le preposizioni

Circa	About
Sopra	
Di fronte a	
A, verso	
Dietro	
Sotto	
Tra, fra	
In	
In basso	
Durante	
Per	
Di	
In	
Davanti	
Dentro	

20. The Prepositions
/ Le preposizioni

Vicino a	Near
Di fianco	
A	
A,sopra	
Fuori	
Sopra	
Per	
Attraverso	
Verso	
Sotto	
Su	
Con	
Senza	
Il gatto è nella scatola	
Il vaso è sulla tavola	
C'è qualcuno alla porta	

21. Giving Directions
/ Dare istruzioni

All'angolo	*At the corner*
Lontano	
Vicino	
Vada dritto	
A sinistra	
A destra	
Giri a sinistra	
Giri a destra	
Vada dritto fino alla prossima strada	
Al semaforo giri a destra	
Come posso giungere a...?	
Dove si trova...?	
Dove si trova la chiesa?	
Il museo si trova vicino al centro commerciale.	
La farmacia è di fronte al palazzo	
Il supermercato si trova vicino al parco.	

22. The Ordinal Numbers
/ I numeri ordinali

Primo	*First*
Secondo	
Terzo	
Quarto	
Quinto	
Sesto	
Settimo	
Ottavo	
Nono	
Decimo	
Undicesimo	
Dodicesimo	
Ventesimo	
Trentesimo	
Il primo palazzo	
Il secondo piano	

23. Countries, Nationalities, and Languages / **Paesi, nazionalità e lingue**

Il brasile	Brazil (Country)
Brasiliano/brasiliana	
Portoghese (lingua)	
La colombia	
Colombiano	
Lo spagnolo	
La cina	
Il cinese	
Il cinese/la cinese	
L'inghilterra	
Inglese	
L'inglese	
La francia	
Il francese / la francese	
Il francese	
La germania	
Tedesco/tedesca	
Il tedesco	
L'italia	

23. Countries, Nationalities, and Languages / Paesi, nazionalità e lingue

Italiano / italiana	Italian
L'italiano	
Il giappone	
Il giapponese / la giapponese	
Il giapponese	
Il messico	
Messicano / messicana	
Lo spagnolo	
La spagna	
Lo spagnolo / la spagnola	
Lo spagnolo	
Gli stati uniti d'america (u.S.A.)	
L'americano / l'americana	
L'inglese	
Di dov'è?	
Sono del brasile	
Io sono brasiliano	
Parlo il portoghese	
Non sono dell'italia	

24. Indefinite Pronouns / **Pronomi indefiniti**

Qualcuno (interrogativo), nessuno (negativo)	*Anybody*
Qualcosa (interrogativo), niente (negativo)	
Nessuno	
Niente	
Qualcuno (affirmativo)	
Qualcosa (affirmativo)	
Tutti	
Tutto	
C'è qalcuno a casa?	
Non voglio niente	
Non è successo niente	
C'è qualcuno nella sala	
Tutto è pronto	

25. The Emotions
/ Le emozioni

Arrabiato	*Angry*
Noioso	
Sicuro di se stesso	
Confuso	
Imbarazzato	
Entusiasmato	
Contento	
Nervoso	
Orgoglioso	
Triste	
Spaventato	
Timido	
Sorpreso	
Preoccupato	
Sono contento / felice	
Lui è triste	
Loro sono sorpresi	
Sei entusiasmato?	
Non sono annoiato	
Lei non è nervosa	
Tutti sono sicuri di se stessi	

26. Adverbs
/ Avverbi

Qualche	A few
Poco	
Molto	
Dopo	
Ancora / Di nuovo	
Prima	
Anche	
Sempre	
Prima	
Sufficentemente	
Ogni giorno	
Esattamente	
Finalmente	
Al primo posto	
Qui	
Tardi	
Più tardi	
Mai	
Prossimo	
Adesso	

26. Adverbs
/ Avverbi

Spesso	Often
Una volta	
Solo	
Fuori	
Davvero	
Proprio qui	
Proprio adesso / subito	
da/da allora	
Lentamente	
Qualche volta	
Presto	
Ancora	
Dopo	
Là	
Oggi	
Domani	
Stasera	
Anche	
Di solito	

27. Auxiliary Verbs
/ Verbi ausiliari

Potere	Can
Potrebbe	
(ausiliare del pasato)	
(ausiliare del presente)	
(ausiliare del presente)	
Dovere	
Potere	
Dovere	
Dovere	
(ausiliari del futuro)	
(ausiliari condizional)	
Puoi venire a cinema?	
Potrebbe darmi cambio?	
Hai lavorato in farmacia?	
Non ho lavorato in farmacia	
Lavori in farmacia?	
Non lavoro in farmacia	
Lui leggi il giornalo?	
Lui non leggi il giornalo	
Devo fare il compito	
Posso aiutarla?	
Devi girare a sinistra	
Dovresti andare dal medico	
Lavoro domani	
Vorrei un bicchiere di vino	

28. Expressions
/ Espressioni

Va bene	All right
S' accomodi	
Venga qui, per favore	
Non ti preoccupare	
Ad esempio	
Buona fortuna!	
Ottima idea!	
Buona giornata!	
Prego,serviti, pure!	
Prego!	
Fai presto!	
Sono d'accordo	
Non sono d'accordo	
Non m'interessa	
Non so.	
Vengo	
Temo che....	
Va bene! D'accordo!	
Stammi bene!	
Lasciami pensare	
Andiamo!	
Subito	
Che bello!	
Certo	
Siediti / Si sieda	
Riguardati!	

29. The Family
/ La famiglia

Italian	English
Il padre	Father
La madre	
Il figlio	
La figlia	
Il fratello	
La sorella	
Il nonno	
La nonna	
Lo zio	
La zia	
Il cugino / lacugina	
Il nipote	
La nipote	
Il marito	
La moglie	
Il fidanzato / il ragazzo	
La fidanzata	
I suoceri	
Il suocero	
La suocera	
Il cognato	
La cognata	
Il patrigno	
La matrigna	
Il fratellastro	
La sorellastra	
Chi è lui?	
Questo è mio fratello	

30. The House
/ La casa

Living room

Il soggiorno

La porta

La finestra

Il divano

La lampada

La sala da pranzo

La tavola

La sedia

La cucina

La stufa

Il forno

Il frigorifero

Il microonde

La camera da letto

Il letto

Il comodino

Il tavolino da toilette

Il comò

Il ripostiglio

La camera da bagno

Lo specchio

Il lavandino

La toilette

La vasca

La lavanderia

Il parcheggio

Dove si trova il soggiorno?

La porta è grande.

La stufa è piccola

La cucina è bella

31. The City
/ La città

Il quartiere	Block
Il palazzo	
La chiesa	
Il cinema	
Il museo	
Il parco	
La farmacia	
Il ristorante	
Il centro commerciale	
Il negozio	
La strada	
Il supermercato	

32. At the Supermarket
/ Al supermercato

Gli alimentari	The food
La frutta	
La mela	
La banana	
La cigliegia	
L'uva	
L'arancia	
La fragola	
I legumi	
I fagioli	
La carota	
Il cavolfiore	
La lattuga	
La cipolla	
Il peperone	
La patata	
Il pomodoro	
La carne	
La carne di manzo	
La carne di pollo	
Il tacchino	
Il prosciutto	
La carne di maiale	
Latticini	
Il burro	
Il formaggio	
Il latte	

32. At the Supermarket
/ Al supermercato

Lo yogurt	Yogurt
La marmellata	
Il pane	
Le uova	
Il pesce	
I frutti di mare	
Le lattine	
Il carrello	
La borsa	
La cesta	
La bottiglia	
La cassa	
Il cassiere/la cassiera	
Servizio clienti	
Le compere	
Quanto ....?	
Quante arance compra?	
Quanto costa?/Quanto costano?	
Quanto costano le banane?	
Voglio....	
Voglio comprare una bottiglia di latte	
Vorrei...	
Vorrei una busta di pomodori....	
Dove sono le lattughe?	
Sono nella sezione uno	
Dove sono le lattine di legumi?	
Sono nella sezioe numero cinque	

33. At the Restaurant
/ Nel ristorante

Il cameriere / la cameriera	Waiter / waitress
La colazione	
Il pranzo	
La cena	
Mangiare	
Bere	
Fare colazione	
Il menù	
Il antipasto	
L'insalata	
La minestra	
Il piatto principale	
La pasta	
Il riso	
Le patate fritte	
Il purea di patate	
Le patate al forno	
Il barbecue	
Pollo fritto	
La bistecca	

33. At the Restaurant
/ Nel ristorante

Il dessert	*Dessert*
Le bevande	
Il caffé	
Il té	
La bevanda gasata	
La limonata	
La spremuta d'arancia	
Le bibite alcoliche	
La birra	
Il vino	
Il conto	
La mancia	
Che cosa desidera?	
Che cosa desidera ordinare?	
Potrebbe darmi il menù, per favore?	
Potrebbe portarmi un po piú d'acqua, per favore?	
Non ho ordinato questo	
Qui il servizio è eccellente	
Il cibo e delizioso!	
Il conto, per favore	
La mancia è compresa	

34. The Office
/ L'ufficio

| Il libro | Book |

Il libro   Book
La calcolatrice
Il computer
La scrivania
Il fax
Il documento
L'armadietto dei documenti
La cartelletta
La tastiera
Lo schermo
Il mouse
L'agenda
Il blocchetto
La carta
La penna
La stampante
Il righelo
Le forbici
Lo schermo
La graffettatrice
Il telefono
Il mio computer non funziona
Non c'è carta nella stampante
Dobbiamo comprare altre cartelle
Non abbiamo una fotocopiatrice

35. Jobs and Positions / Posti di lavoro e finzioni

Il ragioniere	Accountant
L'architetto	
L'attore	
Il capo cuoco	
L'impiegato/l'impiegata	
Il cuoco/la cuoca	
Il dottore	
L'ingegnere	
Il giardiniere	
Designer graffico	
L'avvocato	
L'infermiera	
Il medico	
Il commesso/la commessa	
La segretaria	
Il agente di sicurezza	
Autista di taxi	
L'insegnante	
Il tecnico	
La guida	
Agente turistico	

36. Job Interview
/ L' Intervista di lavoro

Fare domanda di lavoro	Apply for a job
La funzione	
L'esperienza	
Cognome	
Nome	
Lavoro a tempo pieno	
Lavoro a tempo parziale	
Curriculum vitae	
Le abilità	
Lavorare/il lavoro	

37. The Transportation
/ Mezzi di trasporto

L'aereo	Airplane
La bicicletta	
L'autobus	
La macchina	
L'elicottero	
La metropolitana	
La motocicletta	
Il treno	
L'autocarro	

38. The Traffic
/ Il Traffico

La fermata dell'autobus	*Bus stop*
Le striscie pedonale	
L'autostrada	
Il distributore di benzina	
L'incrocio	
La corsia	
Vicolo ceco	
A senso unico	
Il pedone	
La velocità	
Il segnale "stop"	
Salire/entrare	
Scendere/uscire	
Pagare l'autostrada	
Il semaforo	
La stazione del treno	
A due sensi	
Inverzione a u	
Precedenza	
Salire in macchina	
Scendere dalla macchina	
Aspettiamo il treno	

39. The Car
/ La macchina

Italian	English
L'acceleratore	Accelerator
La batteria	
Il cofano	
Il freno	
La frizione	
Il motore	
Il paraurto	
La scatola del cambio	
Le luci	
Lo spechietto retrovisore	
La marca	
Il modello	
Il radiatore	
Il volante	
Il sedile	
Il pneumatico	
Il baule	
La ruota	
Parabrezza	
I tergicristalli	
La macchina ha subito un gusto	
Ho la ruota bucata	
Ho bisogno di una nuova batteria	
Che anno è prodotta la macchina"	
Di quale marca è la macchina?	
Di che modello è la macchina?	
Quante miglia ha la macchina?	

40. Phone Conversations / Conversazioni telefoniche

Telefonare / chiamare	*Call*
Fare il numero	
L'elenco telefonico	
L'informazione	
Il numero interno	
Stia in linea, prego / un attimo, per favore	
Vorrei parlare con...	
Le passo.....	
Passare la telefonata	
Chiamo per....	
Aspetti un attimo	
Lasciare un messaggio	
Mi lasci vedere....	
Chiamare	
Numero telefonico	
Squillo	
Parlare	
Sono io	
Prendere un messaggio	
Parlare	
Parla / chiama....	
Chi parla?	

41. At the Post Office
/ Nell'Ufficio postale

La posta aerea	*Air mail*
Lo sportello	
La busta	
La lettera	
La corrispondenza/la posta	
Il pacco	
La cartolina	
Il postino	
Francobollo	
Inviare	
Consegnare	
La consegna	
Ritirare	
Indirizzo	
Voglio inviare una lettera	
Vorrei ritirare un pacco	
Quanto costano i francobolli?	
Vendete cartoline?	

42. At the Bank
/ Alla banca

Conto	Account
Bancomat	
Estratto conto	
Cassiere/cassiera	
Soldi in contanti	
Il libretto degli assegni	
Il conto corrente	
La carta di credito	
La carta del bancomat	
La ricevuta di deposito	
Il deposito di risparmio	
Depositare	
Risparmiare	
Trasferire	
Prelevare	
La transazione	
Lo scontrino di prolievo	
Vorrei fare un deposito	
Lei ha un conto di risparmio?	
Ho un conto corrente	
Quale è il numero della sua carta di credito?	
Non ho una carta per bancomat	
Dove sono i moduli per il versamento?	

43. At the Airport
/ All'aeroporto

L'arrivo — Arrival

Il corridoio

La dogana

La partenza

La destinazione

L'entrata

L'uscita

La prima classe

Il volo

Il terminale

L'ufficio immigrazioni

Il bagaglio

Il passaporti

Le toilette

La valigia

Arrivare

Partire

Viaggiare

Il viaggio

Dove va?

Posso vedere il suo biglietto, per favore?

Mi fa vedere il suo passaporto, per favore?

Il numero del mio volo è

Dov'è il numero del terminale

L'aereo arriva in ritardo

L'aereo arriva in orario

44. At the Hotel
/ All'albergo

Italian	English
Una camera doppia	Double room
Una camera singola	
La reception	
Il facchino	
L'ascensore	
La ricezione	
Il ricezionista/la ricezionista	
La prenotazione	
Le scale	
La piscina	
L'agenzia turistica	
Il servizio di parcheggio	
La registrazione	
Pagare il conto dell'albergo	
Vorrei fare una prenotazione	
Voglio una camera singola	
Vorrei registrarmi	

45. The Clothes
/ L'abbigliamento

Bathing suit

Il costume da bagno	
La cintura	
La camicetta	
Il cappotto	
Il vestito	
I guanti	
Il cappello	
La giacca	
I pantaloni	
La borsa	
La sciarpa	
La camicia	
Le scarpe	
I pantaloncini corti	
La gonna	
Le calze	
Il completo	
La valigia	
La taglia	
Piccolo	
Medio	
Grande	
Le taglie grandi	

46. At the Shopping Center / Al centro commerciale

Italian	English
Grande magazzino	Department store
Donne	
Uomini	
Giovani	
Bambini	
Reparto donne	
La gioilleria	
Il camerino	
L'ascensore	
La scala mobile	
Posso aiutarla?	
Sto cercando....	
Sto guardando..	
Dov'è il camerino?	
Mi va bene	
Non mi va bene	
Posso pagare qui?	
Voglio cambiare questo	
Vorrei restituire questo	
Mi piace/mi piacciono	
Questa camicetta mi piace	
Non mi piace/non mi piacciono	
Questi pantaloni non mi piacciono	

47. At the Drugstore
/ Alla farmacia

Il disinfettante	Antiseptic
Il cerotto	
L'antibiotico	
L'aspirina	
La fascia	
Medicinale per raffreddore	
Sciroppo per tosse	
I medicinali	
La pomata	
Medicinali da banco	
Analgetico	
Le pastiglie	
La ricetta medica	
Le pillole	
Il termometro	
Il cotone	

48. The Parts of the Body
/ Le parti del corpo umano

La caviglia	Ankle
La mano	
La schiena	
Il sedere	
Il polpaccio	
Il petto	
Il gomito	
I piedi	
Il dito	
Il piede	
Il braccio	
La mano	
La testa	
Il fianco	
Il ginocchio	
La gamba	
Il collo	
La spalla	
Lo stomaco	
La coscia	
Il dito del piede	
La vita	
Il polso	

49. Health Problems
/ Problemi di salute

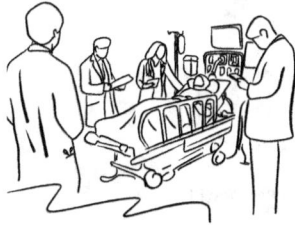

Dolore alla schiena	Backache
Il raffreddore	
La febbre	
Fa male	
Cattiva digestione	
La ferita	
Il dolore	
Il polso	
Malato	
Lo starnuto	
Mal di gola	
Mal di denti	
Ho mal di testa	
Ho mal di stomaco	
Mi fa male il ginocchio	
Mi sono fatto male alla mano	
Ho preso un raffreddore	
Mi fa male la gamba	

50. The Animals
/ Gli animali

L'orso	Bear
L'uccello	
Il gatto	
Il pollo	
La mucca	
Il cane	
L'anatra	
L'elefante	
Il pesce	
Il cavallo	
La lucertola	
Il leone	
La scimmia	
Il topolino	
Il topo	
La tigre	

QUICK LANGUAGES

MULTI-LANGUAGE PHRASEBOOK COLLECTION

SPEAK ANY LANGUAGE NOW!

QUICK LANGUAGES PHRASEBOOK COLLECTION
AVAILABLE TITLES

1. ENGLISH-SPANISH & SPANISH-ENGLISH
2. ENGLISH-ITALIAN & ITALIAN-ENGLISH
3. ENGLISH-FRENCH & FRENCH-ENGLISH
4. ENGLISH-GERMAN & GERMAN-ENGLISH
5. ENGLISH-PORTUGUESE & PORTUGUESE-ENGLISH
6. ENGLISH-CHINESE & CHINESE-ENGLISH
7. ENGLISH-ARABIC & ARABIC-ENGLISH
8. ENGLISH-JAPANESE & JAPANESE-ENGLISH
9. ENGLISH-KOREAN & KOREAN-ENGLISH
10. ENGLISH-RUSSIAN & RUSSIAN-ENGLISH
11. ENGLISH-TURKISH & TURKISH-ENGLISH

GET THE AUDIOVISUAL AND
INTERACTIVE CONTENT AT
QuickLanguages.com